Contents

Introduction

Foreword

Introduction

Grand Designs with Flowers has been produced by the Education Committee to celebrate the 50th Anniversary of the National Association of Flower Arrangement Societies (NAFAS).

As we look back on the history of flower arranging, we know past eras have always produced grand designs to suit the requirements of the age. Today, floral artists are being challenged to produce bigger and better, faster and more economical designs for every imaginable occasion.

The roots of my family for the last ten generations have been firmly established in London, and as a child, although a visit 'up home' as we called it was an exciting event, I easily recall the devastation following the war years. The poverty and degradation were appalling, but there

Photos: Katherine Kear

was a resilience to survive. My lasting memories of those times are the flowers, mainly geraniums that decorated the balconies, terraces, back yards and churches. The local florist was important to everyone and I was often sent by my grandmother to order a bouquet, wreath or just a small bunch of flowers for the War Memorial outside St Mary's Church, Somers Town.

Janet James   Photo: Chrissie Harten

This was the dawn of a new start for flower arrangers, florists and gardeners following the Second World War. Perhaps this was where my love of flowers and flower arranging began and developed. When I joined a Flower Club in 1978 I little imagined I would become the Chairman of such a prestigious association as NAFAS and writing the introduction to this book.

Photographs of arrangements from the early days of NAFAS make us appreciate how far we have developed in fifty years. The individual

Margaret Thomas   Photo: Chrissie Harten

authors of each chapter in this book are experts in 'Grand Designs' and I commend to you their information, skill and advice in making every large scale design special.

I record my thanks to the authors for their valuable contributions, to the Education Committee for the two years of hard work in producing this book, and last, but by no means least, to the Editor, Katherine Kear, whose vision with words and photographs has led to the production of a very special handbook, full of 'grand' ideas.

**Valerie Best
National Chairman
2007–2009**

*Elizabeth Graham
Photo: Chrissie Harten*

Foreword

NAFAS was granted charitable status in 1984 due to its educational activities. One such activity is to publish leaflets and books that help tutors and students to pursue their art. All the contributors to this book are experienced teachers, competitors, exhibitors and demonstrators who have used their extensive knowledge of floral art to prepare their chapter.

The National Education Committee of NAFAS encourages its members and the general public to develop their skills in floral art and related subjects and to this end it organises the NAFAS Certificates in Floral Art & Design and the Home Study Course.

Everyone who is involved in floral art knows that floral designs can be of any size; compare the exquisite miniatures and petites at our National shows with the voluptuous arrangements for a royal wedding. Each arrangement has its own design criteria to be executed by the skilled floral artist. This book concentrates on Grand Designs, designs for large areas, religious venues, stately homes, marquees, public places and the open air. There is a chapter devoted to large-scale mechanics illustrating the 'make it

'At last I've got it!'
Photo: unknown

Oxfordshire Federation WI
Photo: Catriona Karney

'Not sure I can stay here too long!'   Photo: unknown

big' technique. Health & Safety is also covered which is most important when dealing with events that involve the public.

Photo: unknown

I am grateful to everyone who has been involved in the preparation of this book, I know it will be an important addition to the floral art teaching library.

Irene Manson
Chairman National Education Committee

Tony Brown

Photo: Chrissie Harten

Large Scale Mechanics

Working on large scale designs often requires the designer to come up with new and ingenious ways of making the flowers appear effortlessly in just the right place often with no visible means of support and mechanics. This may require a lot of forward planning and several visits to timber merchants and DIY shops. It is also important, on a practical level, that the mechanics are not too bulky as often the flowers, foliage and mechanics have to be transported by personal cars rather than commercial vehicles and more often, carried a distance when setting up.

Here are some ideas and hints towards making individual mechanics; some are relatively simple to construct, however, they provide the beginnings of understanding how to create mechanics for large-scale designs. They are set out in an easy to follow format and all of them will be able to be taken down and transported with ease.

Clever with Angles

Materials: woodblock
                  stand

This first mechanic is a block of wood that can be used to angle anything in any direction and can be adjusted in size to fit its purpose. Care will need to be taken to ensure that the choice of a larger block does not upset the balance of the mechanic overall.

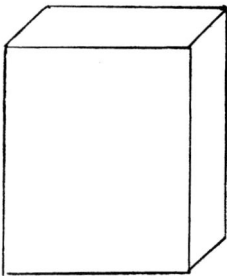

Draw shape   *Cut out dark area*   *Complete shape*

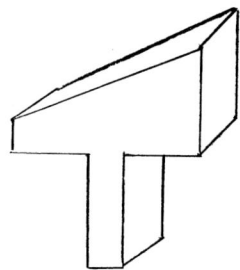

This block when prepared is put onto a lamp stand, or similar with a hollow centre, the stand will need to have a reasonably sized hollow centre to enable the 'leg' of the block to be thick enough to support the head. The stand will need a solid base for balance.

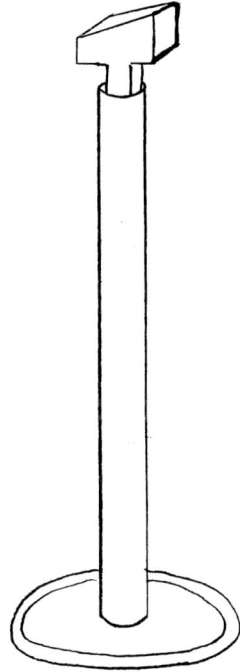

A pedestal can also be used by taking the top out so that the stand is left. Cut the angle out of a block of wood, but do not cut out a 'leg'. A deeper piece of wood will be needed this time to allow for the block to be turned over and a hole needs to be drilled just slightly larger than the top of the pedestal-about 2-3 inches. For a more permanent fixing, glue can be used in the hole for security.

A container or accessory
can easily be attached to
the wood.

Altar Vase

Materials: length of square or round wood, remember, measure before
cutting and allow an extra half inch on the height
a broom handle would work but check circumference
few screws or nails
piece of flat wood approx 4ins square

The first length of wood needs to fit snugly in the opening of the vase,
cut to the height of the vase plus half an inch. The second piece has
to be flat and is nailed or screwed to the top of the first piece. If the
container used is delicate then a rubber pad can be used on the base of
the pole. The mechanic is then inserted into the vase. Place a dish and
foam on the shelf thus enabling a larger design to be used on the vase.

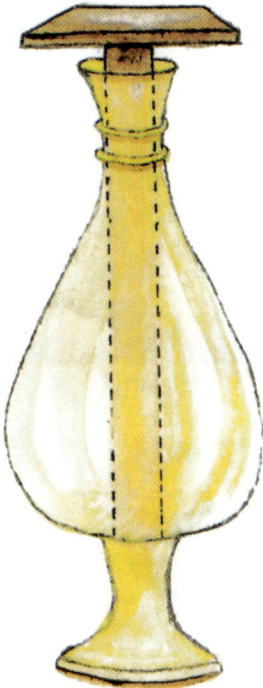

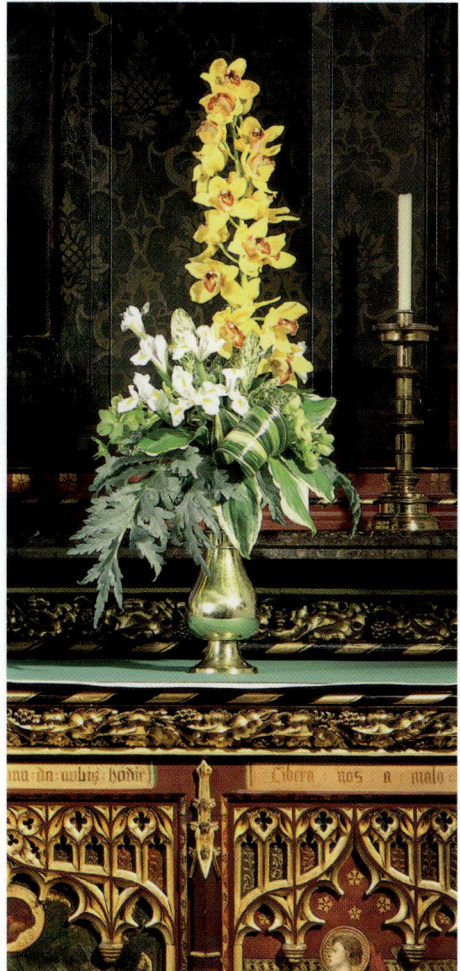

John Chennell
Photo: Lyndon Parker

ARCHWAY

Materials: 6 large angle brackets plus screws
2 lengths 5x5cm sq wood for the sides
pipe lagging to required length
hazel or *willow* branches, these must be thick and pliable

To assemble:

1. Screw 3 angle brackets to one end of each of the wood lengths.
2. Wind the *willow* or *hazel* on to the top and end about 30cm down.
3. Stand the wood up and then bend the *willow* or *hazel* so that they overlap in the middle, you may need an extra pair of hands for this.
4. With the arch in place cover the *willow* or *hazel* with the lagging so that it is thicker and better able to hold the foam.
5. Cut blocks of foam into quarter lengths and tape on as much as you think you will need to do the work. Tape in place.
6. Starting with the foliage and using one variety at a time work it all over evenly before adding the next, (the choice of foliage will depend on event and season, shorter more robust foliages will work better).
7. Repeat in a similar fashion with the flowers, it is surprising how little is needed but how effective the result.

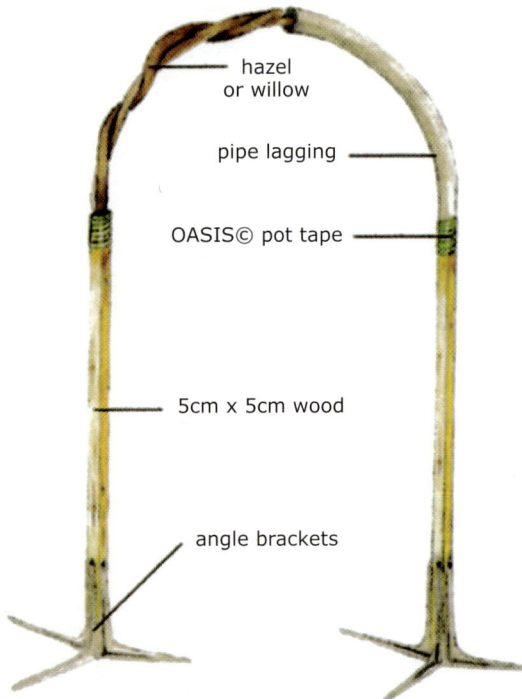

hazel
or willow

pipe lagging

OASIS© pot tape

5cm x 5cm wood

angle brackets

John Chennell   Photo: Lyndon Parker

Versatile Metal

This is a versatile construction made from metal, it can be made fairly large, however, it can easily be broken down for transportation in a car. An impressive overall size is 14ft x 6ft needing a base that is wide or heavy enough for safety. The rest breaks down into 7 pieces, which are:

Materials: 2 poles
            4 arms with dishes to hold the foam
            1 top plate to hold foam

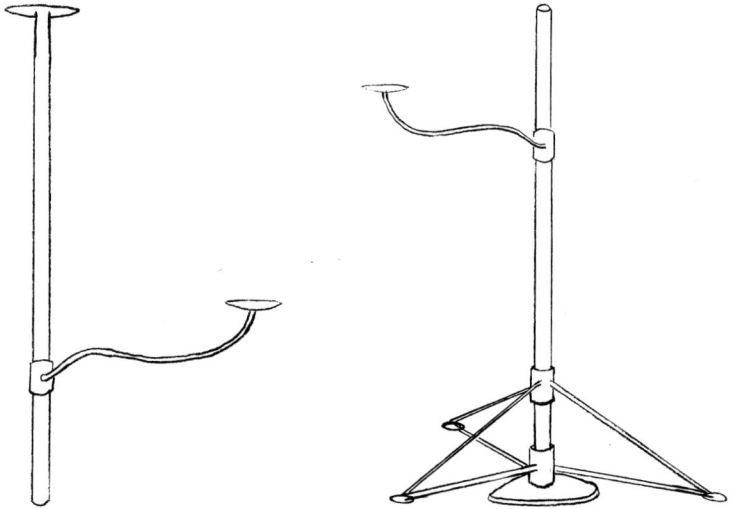

A mechanic like this can be designed to suit individual requirements and a sketch can be worked upon to include a solid base plate for stability, as well as the base illustrated, arms of varied shape and length with plates at the end for dishes. The components can be screwed together or have interlocking junctions. Whilst this needs specialist construction anyone can design their own creation to suit the event.

Herbaceous Borders

Materials: 4 pieces of wood cut to the length required
            wooden base with optional wood blocks as feet
            screws or nails

This is a simple and effective way of creating a garden type design and an herbaceous border is a good example to use. Decide on the size of the border, this will then provide the measurements for the 4 pieces of wood that are to be nailed or screwed together to make a square, or what ever shape is chosen, with the wooden base attached at the bottom as the floor. If blocks are needed as feet it is better to attach these first before the floor is put in making sure there are enough feet for stability. The next and most important stage is to use a strong plastic sheet to line it. Having made sure that the lining is watertight floral foam is added and then the border can be brought to life.

Metal and Wood Combinations

This mechanic allows a series of smaller designs to be made vertically and taken away from the floor area.

Materials: metal base plate with pole
2 Lengths of wood
wing nuts and screws

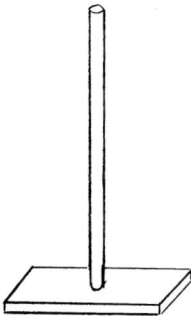

The main piece of this mechanic is a heavy metal plate with a fixed rod or screw attachment, this is to give strength and stability, and can be as tall, as simple or complicated as necessary.

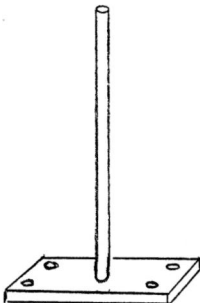

Holes can be put into the base and the whole thing screwed to a larger base if further stability is needed.

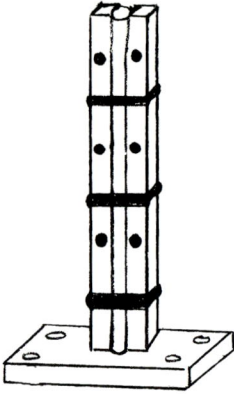

The 2 lengths of wood are attached vertically to each side of the pole, cable ties are a good idea. Next, holes are drilled where necessary to support containers or accessories on the upright. Wing nuts are a good idea to attach the containers and accessories. They do not require a screwdriver and will make for a simpler take down.

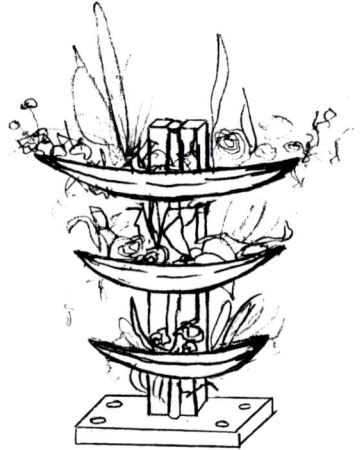

The design illustrated has used spathes as containers, however anything that can be attached to the upright can be used.

Flat and Low

Materials for a 3ft (90cm) design: 3 ft length of black plastic guttering
2 end downpipe junctions
2 caps from black spray-paint cans, or any black tops
4 plastic frogs

N.B. If longer than1m the guttering tends to sag. If a longer design is needed a middle down pipe junction will be required, use one more can cap and an extra 0.80cm piece of guttering. By using this concept the length can be increased indefinitely.

1. Attach the 2 end downpipe junctions to the end of the guttering.
2. The 2 spray can caps are used to seal off the downpipes. Fix them to the downpipes.
3. Space the 4 plastic frogs evenly along the guttering and glue in position.
4. Be creative with this design, the mechanics can be used for a flat church window ledge or the front of a choir stall or ... the list goes on.

John Chennell   *Photo: Lyndon Parker*

Flowers for All in Public Places

'Open to the use or enjoyment of all' is the dictionary definition of a public place, 'public' being the major consideration when an invitation to stage floral designs has been received!

A public place can range from an art gallery, museum, theatre, educational establishment or hotel, to a civic or military building or even an outdoor space (this is dealt with in the Outdoor chapter). It naturally follows that there will be a great passage of people, the majority of whom will be unfamiliar with large floral designs suddenly invading a familiar location. It is important that there is no interference with the functionality of the rooms within the venue, designs should enhance a setting, create atmosphere and cause visual excitement, but in no way obstruct the route the public follows or the role the venue serves. Health and safety factors will be a major consideration within a public place where large numbers of people are present, and therefore every endeavour should be made to place designs in unobtrusive sites and levels. Health and safety is covered in its own chapter.

Once a venue has been identified and the atmosphere of the surroundings absorbed following an initial viewing, it will be necessary to know who will be funding the event, so an early in-depth meeting is vital between the venue representative and the floral designer. Quite often a public building is made available free of charge for charitable purposes, therefore the charity representative must be able to participate in the plans.

Important questions need to be raised:

- Is there a budget for the flowers? It is usual and it is a good idea to adhere to the sum quoted since there is nothing to be gained by spending more than the allowance.
- Being a public place, does public liability insurance cover all eventualities, together with cover for furnishings and fittings?
- Can out-of-hours opening times be available for staging and dismantling the floral designs and also for their maintenance, is there a ready supply of water?
- Can use be made of existing containers and artefacts?
- Would it be better to focus designs in areas or adjacent to works of art that are popular and positive with the public, yet placed outside 'touching' distance?
- Can spotlighting be deployed if necessary?
- Is storage space available for buckets and flowers?

Sue
Blandford
Photo:
Chrissie
Harten

Wessex and Jersey Area   *Photo: Ted Stewart*

- Is there to be a Preview (which is recommended as this is where the charity raises a lot of money) and can a place be set-aside for the serving of drinks and a buffet, or will trays be offered around?

- Has the full value of press coverage and publicity been determined? Charities are often helpful on this matter and their own budgets include money for this.

Building Style

The type of building will determine the style of the designs. Modern/contemporary architecture suggests restraint, and like a floral design there will always be areas of greater and lesser interest, allowing the eye to move around the structure from all angles.

In a contemporary building with a lot of glass and metal, minimal use of plant material is necessary with bold, strong lines. These are achievable with *Cornus*, *Bamboo*, *Salix* (fasciated and contorted) and bold flowers such as *Hydrangea*, *Allium*, *Anthurium*, *Eremurus*, *Gerbera*, *Helianthus* and *Hippeastrum*.

Traditional public buildings require mass designs with richer flowers such as the *Rose*, *Lily*, *Peony*, *Nerine*, *Delphinium* and *Cymbidium* orchids. Classical architecture needs to be complemented by large lavish designs and possibly with the addition of ornate swags and garlands.

Importance must be given to the compatibility of a design within a setting and staging a design in situ will ensure this. There must be harmony between components, rhythm and repetition of colour, scale and proportion and forms and texture in order to enhance the setting and create atmosphere.

Ninon Linnell and Barbara Bowman
Photo: Allen Rout

21

Jean Crane

Photo: Ted Stewart

Mo Duffill

Photo: Mo Duffill

Warnings!

Having considered the whole ambience of the situation, the following obvious practical design factors emerge:

- A design placed too high could give maintenance problems
- Accessories need to be considered, they can be misappropriated, instead tell the story with plant material – colours and textures are invaluable here
- Due to the passage of people there must be total stability in a design, if in doubt add extra weight such as pin holders, sand or gravel to the vase
- Use fireproofed materials where appropriate
- Avoid unpleasant smelling materials, prickly or stinging ones
- Use large, deep containers to hold ample water to prolong plant life and also leave space for watering
- Containers, if visible, should be in keeping with the period and setting
- Do take the compatibility of the individual arranger or design group into account, think about their skills and personality for working together!

Do your Homework

When providing floral designs within a museum, art gallery or alternative period setting remember that it is beneficial to spend time in studying the style and history behind the particular subject to gain a better understanding and be in empathy with it. To have studied the relevant NAFAS course on period history is a bonus, there are two NAFAS books *The Guide to Period Flower Arranging* and the *NAFAS Period Guide II*, which are an invaluable resource.

Researching a story behind a work of art is important. Visit the venue, tour the route the public will take and end up in the shop where catalogues and postcards can be purchased of artefacts, engravings, tapestries and sculptures. Anything visual to be studied in a quiet moment is important, as cameras are generally not allowed to be used in such buildings for security reasons.

Henry Moore sculpture

Photo: Don Manson

Inspiration

Flower arranging is a three-dimensional art often influenced by two-dimensional art forms such as painting and photography. Inspiration for both modern and traditional work can be drawn from works by famous painters, sculptors and architects. Sculpture provides the arranger with the principles for the three-dimensional aspect of a work. Nature is a great influencing factor in designs due to its varied patterns, shapes and colours. A designer could specifically view a Barbara Hepworth sculpture and observe her use of plastic rods, string and wire to create linear patterns and be similarly inspired to use reeds, grasses and bleached rattan cane to emulate strings.

© Tate London. Artist: Dame Barbara Hepworth
Stringed Figure (Curlew) Version 11, 1956.
Bowness, Hepworth Estate

A Henry Moore sculpture could be replicated using driftwood or hollowed-out sections of a tree trunk as the main component.

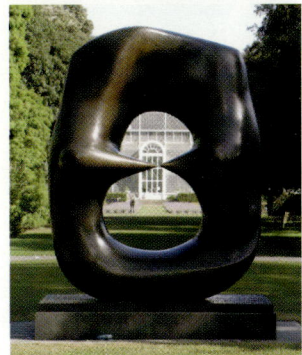

Henry Moore sculpture
Photo: Don Manson

25

Dramatic plant material can convey sculptural dominance and flowers added for contrast become secondary. They are often omitted completely and the design is achieved with sculptural forms of plant material with space, rhythm and depth.

Such works of art in public places, viewed all round, will have design limitations for disguising mechanics, but this can be overcome by concealing the mechanics in such a way that they become an integrated part of the design or, if a container is to be visible, its colour and style must be in keeping with the design. To use valuable containers owned by the venue, written rather than oral permission should be obtained, as the onus will be on the arranger to preserve and protect an object d'art

Tips: Place a bowl inside a period or valuable container
Never use wire netting near silver
Avoid the use of floral fix
Test container to ensure it holds water before the event

The Art Gallery

An invitation to create a floral design in this venue is a challenge and requires a concentrated observation of paintings to establish where a complementary design should be placed, focussing on something positive or popular with the public or area. Against a landscape painting, nature, due to its large variety of shapes, colours, textures and patterns is a great influencing factor and can be portrayed by restrained use of plant materials such as lichened branches, leaves, moss and cones for woodland or moorland and bulrushes, iris and stone for water features.

Bob Harris   *Photo: Katherine Kear*

Jean Lock *Photo: Margaret Coates*

A Still Life painting, with its carefully arranged fruits and objects of differing shapes and sizes, can be a great source of inspiration for the flower arranger on composition, placement and colour in the design, and the viewing public will find these two related forms, art and floral art, easily understandable and visibly interesting to study and enjoy.

Due to having no recognisable subject matter, an abstract or modern art depiction demands restraint and the use of strong stems, both straight and curved, i.e. dried hogweed, stripped branches, fasciated willow and palm spathes. Perspex is a useful aid in abstract flower arranging due to its unobtrusiveness.

Civic and Military

The floral designer staging in a civic or military building for some special event will, for the most part, have to concentrate on colour, these colours may be applicable to a regiment's own colours and, in a civic building with its importance to the local community and a pride in heritage and tradition, there may be colours associated with a Council's logo or an aspect of local industry. In such settings, additional placements of plaques and Coats of Arms, ideally replicated using dried plant materials, could be introduced and effectively achieved if there is ample wall space but little floor-level space. One bold structure in a high-ceilinged room as a focal point, using large bold forms and textured leaves is all that will be required.

Jennifer Walters

Photo: Lyndon Parker

All Those Other Places!

An educational establishment's open day or prize giving ceremony will generally require a large floral design in the foyer or to the rear of a platform, so as to be unobtrusive yet as a colourful backdrop as students come forward to be handed their certificates. The colours of the school will invariably be requested, or it will be left to the arranger to produce a flamboyant pedestal design to enhance the setting with impact. Cultivating the co-operation of the caretakers will always be a good move as they will be an invaluable source of knowledge as to where items can be stored, where to find the water supply, rubbish bin availability and any other queries.

Margaret Coates   Photo: Margaret Coates

A hotel foyer is a busy, bustling place. In a large city hotel, contract florists are generally employed to produce a large vase or container of water holding bold flowers of restful neutral colours and large leaves such as *Kentia* palms, *Aspidistra*, *Phormium*, etc., often placed on a tall plinth in a central position as a welcome to guests and without any danger of toppling over and causing an accident. In country hotels and inns the atmosphere is more informal and relaxed, and garden flowers and flowering shrubs supplemented with 'florist's flowers' can be arranged in traditional containers, to be in keeping with a more homely ambience.

And So to The Clear Up

Wherever and whatever the building, a date and time will have been arranged to dismantle the floral designs, and it is at this point that a decision will already have been made as to what happens to the surviving flowers and foliage. Individual organisations that have invited arrangers to create the designs may have their own requests, however, it is important that the venue is left as it was found and sad, old flowers taken home with the rest of the rubbish.

Religious Venues

The grandeur, splendour and spaciousness of religious venues create the arena, atmosphere and capacity for many of our distinct sacred and secular community occasions. Floral designs within these settings provide a natural link between the church and the community which it serves. Plant material has been associated with traditional customs and ceremonies for centuries as an outward sign of creation and new life.

At special occasions throughout the calendar year flowers add to the splendour and dignity, changing the ambience and bringing the beauty of the natural world into the heart of the building to enhance acts of worship. Flower festivals in particular encourage accessibility, drawing people into the venue where the grace of the floral artistry inspires and uplifts, uniting all in joyful thanksgiving for creation.

As floral artists in a modern age, we are privileged to be able to use our hands, hearts and minds to contribute our own offerings through the special medium of plant material, remembering that the house was first created by past artisans and craftsmen to glorify their Creator.

During the past fifty years, members of NAFAS Flower Clubs have used their creative skills to organise and implement innumerable Flower Festivals and other major events in religious venues throughout the United Kingdom and overseas. These events have brought immense pleasure to members of local communities, both visually and spiritually. Revenue raised has contributed large amounts of funding for renovation and refurbishment projects of cathedrals and churches as well as to the work of many worthy charitable organisations.

For flower arrangers the experience is truly stimulating and inspirational as floral designs are created to harmonise and complement the magnificence of the venue's architecture and furnishings. The team effort involved brings designers closer together, forging and renewing friendships through the medium of flowers.

The uplifting sense of achievement which each personal gift of talent and energy contributes to the overall magnificence of the occasion.

The 4 C's –
Consultation, co-ordination,
co-operation and communication

- Before any large-scale event takes place in a religious venue, meticulous attention to detailed planning is essential for success, well in advance of the occasion.

Lydney and Severnside Flower Club

Photo: Veronica Coe

Charlton Kings Flower Club   *Photo: Veronica Coe*

Nailsworth and District Flower Arrangement Society   Photo: Veronica Coe

- A management committee comprising, as a minimum, chairman, secretary, treasurer, designer and publicity officer must be established as soon as a special event is inaugurated. This must incorporate official representatives from the venue, representatives from any charities that may benefit from the event, (these may have good contacts) as well as flower-arranging experts. All members must have a clear view of their individual role through identified terms of reference.

- Many cathedrals and churches are Grade 1 listed buildings, decoration therefore may involve consultation with conservation organisations such as English Heritage.

- Dates and times of the event opening, staging and dismantling must be decided at the outset to fit into the religious calendar, also bearing in mind the cost of flowers at certain times of the year and other relevant local and national events.

- The methods of financing the requirements of the event must be clearly defined with consideration given to how the accounts will be managed. It is helpful to organisers if a good proportion of funding can be available prior to the occasion for the purchase of flowers, special mechanics, publicity, brochures, etc.

- Funding may be raised through sponsorship, donations, loans, grants, fundraising activities and sale of goods, special preview events

Dursley and District Flower Society   *Photo: Veronica Coe*

and entrance fees. These entrance fees may be gift-aided and VAT reclaimed on the purchase of flowers and other materials.

- It is desirable to decide how any proceeds will be distributed after the event.

- Consultation and communication between the Chapter, religious leaders, flower guild and other staff of the venue and the floral designers is absolutely essential throughout the planning and staging processes. All parties should have a flexible approach, as plans may need to change in the event of unforeseen circumstances.

Designing and Placement of Floral Designs

- A floral designer with expertise in planning and staging large-scale designs must be appointed to the management committee of this event at the outset. This person should have a wide knowledge of different styles of design and be capable of managing the designers who will construct the arrangements.

- The wishes of the clergy in the placements of designs must be respected. Some incumbents prefer plant material not to be placed, for example, on an altar or font.

Katherine Kear   Photo: Katherine Kear

Arranger unknown   *Photo: Veronica Coe*

- The designer's role is to develop an overall theme and sub-themes, which generally involves the creation of interpretative designs. The theme may be selected by the church, the arrangers or both, but should be approved by all involved at an early stage.

- Consideration when developing the designs should be given to the time of year, the choice of plant materials, the available budget, the level of ability of the arrangers and local events and customs.

- Designs should be planned to enhance the beauty of the fabric of the venue and not to hide it. Designs can be raised or hung so that they are easily visible from a distance.

- The designs must be in scale with the setting, which will inevitably mean large designs or groupings, large-scale containers, plant materials and other artefacts.

- Linking form and colour of designs to existing fabric and furnishings such as stained glass, carvings, tapestries, etc. can help to create overall harmony.

- Lighting in many ecclesiastical buildings is often inadequate, and consideration should be given to the colour of each design in this respect or the introduction of temporary lighting systems.

- Decisions should be made on an appropriate route through the venue, so that variations in style, interpretation and colour create interest for visitors.

Tenbury Wells Flower Club   *Photo: Veronica Coe*

- Each venue and each occasion is unique. The design team should walk through the proposed route to determine viewpoints, linking from one area to another both conceptually and visually.

Practical Considerations

- The movement of visitors within the building at large scale events must be considered to avoid congestion, with suitable routes and methods of crowd control carefully planned.

- A risk assessment should be undertaken to ensure that proposed placements do not obstruct fire exits or constitute any additional hazard.

- The wishes of the clergy should always be respected with regard to the placement of floral designs.

- The placement of stands, containers and plant material must not impede movement, particularly of the clergy as they perform their duties.

- Furnishings and fabric of the building must be protected from damage; additional supports for designs must not damage any part of the wood or stonework, and floors and furniture must be protected from water spillage and scratching.

Jean Hughes
Photos: Mike Price

A simple ratchet
strap makes
a pillar design
possible.

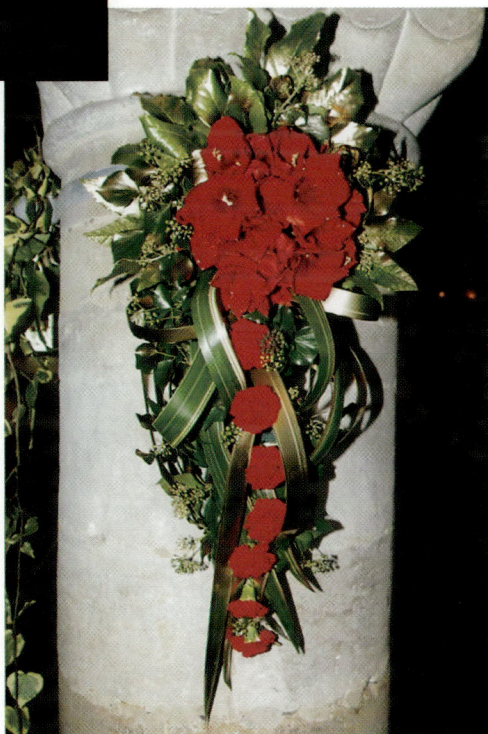

- All stands and other mechanics must be secure and firmly based; if necessary secure with additional wire or other means of support to prevent any arrangement falling over.

- Existing furniture may often be removed to create more space, but movement and storage of this is an important consideration.

- If designs are placed high in the building they will not be obstructed by standing visitors and will be highly visible.

- Within the team of arrangers there should be suitable talent and skills to implement each exhibit.

- There must be a substantial rota of stewards for both staging and open days, who are fully briefed to perform their role efficiently. Stewards should be clearly identified through special uniform, sashes or badges.

- The location of water and water containers for soaking foam and conditioning plant material should be convenient or suitable hawsers/pipes installed.

- Arrangements must be made to dispose of organic and non-organic waste in an appropriate manner, both during staging and dismantling.

Feasts, Festivals and Events in the Christian Church Calendar

It is customary to decorate religious venues with flowers and foliage for many of the feasts and festivals that occur throughout the Church's year. Specific colours are traditionally associated with these occasions, and are seen in vestments of the clergy, altar frontals and other textiles. The floral designs created to enhance the occasion should be selected to harmonise with these colours.

Advent
Preparation for the birth of Christ at Christmas
In many venues no flowers are used
Colour – purple or violet

Christmas
Celebration of the birth of Christ
Evergreens are important to represent eternal life. Even today some churches do not allow mistletoe inside the building.
Holly and ivy berries represent fertility
Colours – gold and white

Epiphany
Celebration of the visit of the Magi to Christ
Colour – white to Candlemass and then green

Katherine Kear   Photo: Mike Price

Lent

A time of penitence
No flowers used and historically decorative items are removed or
covered, especially during Holy week where crosses are veiled in purple.
Colour – purple or violet, unbleached linen often used

Palm Sunday

Celebration of Christ's entry into Jerusalem
A parade of palm leaves often occurs followed by the spreading of
palms in the aisle of the church or cathedral. Palm crosses given to
congregation

Good Friday

Crucifixion of Christ
No flowers
Colour – Black or purple

Easter Day

Resurrection of Christ and triumph of life over death
Joyous celebration using an abundance of flowers
Many venues have a decorative Easter Garden with tomb and stone
Colours – gold and white

Ripon Cathedral Easter Garden
Pat Hutchinson
Photo: Pat Hutchinson

Pentecost (Whit Sunday)

Coming of the gift of the Holy Spirit
Colour red

Harvest Festival

Thanksgiving for the harvest
Decoration with fruit, vegetables, bread and sheaves of corn

Remembrance Day

Remembrance of those who died serving their country in war
Traditionally evergreen foliage and red poppies; wreaths and crosses

Other special events could include:

Ordination or installation of Priests
Consecration of Bishops and new churches
Saints Days
Mothering Sunday
Baptism, Confirmation, Weddings and Funerals

Buddhist Festivals

There does not appear to be evidence of 'grand occasions' taking place in Buddhist temples, but throughout the year celebrations of events in Buddha's life take place. These are joyful and happy occasions, where devotees bring gifts of flowers, candles and incense to place at the feet of Buddha in gratitude for his life and teachings. Some festivals are specific to a particular country, but all Buddhists celebrate the Wesak or Buddha Day universally.

The festival of Wesak takes place annually on the date of the full moon in May, to celebrate the day on which Buddha was born, received enlightenment and died. It provides an opportunity for members of the Buddhist community to re-affirm their commitment to their spiritual journey towards enlightenment.

Buddhist shrines in temples are beautifully decorated with offerings of vegetarian

Photo: Katherine Kear

Photo: Katherine Kear

food, flowers, lanterns and candles, which represent the transience of life as they are subject to decay and destruction. However, it is a joyful and colourful event, incorporating the ceremony of bathing the Buddha, when scented water from a basin decorated with flowers is poured over the statue.

Buddhists respect the innate beauty of flowers, which are considered an exemplar of the uniqueness yet interconnectedness of all life. Followers offer the lotus, regarded as a sacred flower in Buddhist culture, representing purity and divine birth, to Buddha at most festivals.

Photo: Katherine Kear

Hindu Festivals

The religion of Hinduism has many festivals throughout the year, including the major festivals of Diwali, Holi, Onam and Durga Puja.

Diwali, the Festival of Light is celebrated through the lunar calendar at the end of October, with hundreds of lights, fireworks, flowers, sweets and worship. It celebrates the victory of good over evil within every human being and the uplifting of spiritual darkness.

The Harvest Festival of Onam takes place in September to celebrate the success of harvest. Superb colourful floral carpets or pookalam are created using flowers, petals, leaves, rice, sugar, ghee, nuts, etc. in symmetric or rangoli patterns at the entrance to temples or courtyards of houses. They consist of ten

Photo: Katherine Kear

45

Photo: Katherine Kear

rings of floral materials representing the ten days of the festival and can reach up to 5 metres in diameter. Today designs are often drafted on a computer before implementation.

Fragrance is an important element in floral decorations; *roses*, *jasmine*, *hibiscus* and other perfumed flowers are threaded onto garlands for decoration of shrines and personal adornment.

Jewish Festivals

A Jewish festival is a day or series of days observed by Jews as a holy or secular commemoration of an important event in Jewish history. There are numerous festivals throughout the year, each with their own customs and traditions, at some of which plant materials are used to decorate the synagogue.

The festival of Shavuot commemorates the day that God gave the Ten Commandments to Moses on Mount Sinai, when it is said that the land blossomed with flowers and vegetation. Homes and synagogues are therefore decorated with plants, flowers and leafy branches as appropriate symbolism. During the celebration in the synagogue, the bimah or elevated platform on which the reading from the Torah is made is covered with a special arch and adorned with flowers and foliage.

The festival of Sukkot, Festival of the Tabernacles, celebrates the fruit harvest occurring in the autumn and recalls God's protection of the Israelites during their wanderings in the wilderness. Temporary shelters or booths of branches are constructed and typically each person collects and binds together four different plant species to be taken to the synagogue. These are *palm*, *willow*, *myrtle* and *citrus*, which represent four different types of personality that exist within a community.

Jewish weddings traditionally incorporate a chuppah, a cloth canopy on four poles, which represents the home that the couple will build together and the presence of God over the covenant of marriage. The four corners of the chuppah are beautifully decorated with choice flowers and foliage.

Muslim Festivals

Muslims have a rich history of celebrating their important festivals. These occasions are celebrated in families within their community, where prayers are offered for being blessed with the opportunity to celebrate the joyous event. There is much rejoicing – buildings are decorated with lights, special food is prepared, and children receive gifts of sweets and money. In the mosques oral renditions of the Koran and poetry are presented to praise Allah and the Prophet Muhammad. However, there is no evidence of floral designs being incorporated into these events.

Secular Events in Religious Venues

Increasingly today, administrators of religious venues are opening their doors to a wider community to utilise the premises for grand secular events. The Cathedral or principal church may often be the largest public building in a city or town and the nave may be transformed to accommodate presentations, civic occasions, graduation ceremonies, music festivals, recitals, choral concerts, jazz concerts, son et lumiere, armed forces presentations, corporate events, art exhibitions and more. These events may require further embellishment with flowers to add grandeur to the occasion or to create a thematic link.

Several Cathedrals regularly remove furniture from the nave to use its spacious capacity for fundraising dinners and events, augmented by floral displays linked to the theme to create a fitting atmosphere.

Ripon Cathedral was used for the European finale of the Entente Florale award ceremony, where 450 delegates from across Europe attended the presentation ceremony. The nave of the Cathedral was transformed by the floral designs into an atmospheric woodland glade with birch trees, shrubs, ferns and tree stumps, together with computer generated music and special lighting effects.

Styles of Design

- Floral designs must be in scale with the overall size of the venue to have impact, large individual arrangements or groupings are essential whereas numerous small placements create an over-elaborate effect.

- The architectural style of the building will often dictate an appropriate overall style, but the designer should be flexible, original and creative in approach.

- Traditional decorative styles have been employed successfully at grand occasions

Rosemary Dixey
Photo: Veronica Coe

Arranger: unknown
Photo: Jenny Bennett

for decades. Still a popular choice, this style often reflects the graceful ambience of the venue. Traditional styles might include large pedestals, columns, urns, garlands, swags, plaques, floral carpets, etc.

- Contemporary styles have the advantage of providing strong structural impact with bold materials and blocked colours. These could include contemporary metal stands of all descriptions, constructions of stems and branches, wire mesh screens, montages, collages, banners, woven figures, floral carpets and many more.

- The majority of large scale events, particularly flower festivals, will incorporate interpretative designs which may depict religious teachings, represent special feasts and festivals associated with the church calendar or may be linked to history, events or personalities within the locality. The designer should research the background of each theme and liaise with both the management team and

Worcester Floral Arrangement Society & Worcester Cathedral Flower Guild
Photo: Veronica Coe

Pershore Flower Club
Photo: Veronica Coe

the flower arrangers to ensure that all are aware of the message to be displayed.

- A skilled designer can create powerful images using plant material to convey messages, which evoke sensitive and spiritual responses in the viewer.

- Large designs staged outside the entrance to the venue will not only provide a welcome to visitors, but will also act as an advertisement of the occasion. Care must be exercised to reduce the impact of damage from weather conditions and potential vandalism or theft.

- The designer must ensure that the building is decorated with good taste and dignity in keeping with the character of the venue.

Margaret Packer, Maureen Gillman, Joyce Armes and Barbara Padbury
Photo: Veronica Coe

Selection of Seasonal Plant Material

- Plant material should be bold to have impact and to be in scale with the setting.

- Advancing colours and colours of high luminosity are advantageous in poor quality lighting.

- All plant material should be well conditioned before use, and the water supply maintained throughout the duration of the event. A team of stewards to water exhibits should be organised.

- Suitable flowers could include:
  Agapanthus, Acanthus, Allium, Amaryllis, Anthurium, Carnation, Chrysanthemum, Dahlia, Delphinium, Digitalis, Gerbera, Gladiolus, Helianthus, Orchid, Peony, Protea, Rose, Rhododendron and *Strelitzia*.

- Suitable foliage could include:
  Aspidistra, Bergenia, Choisya, Cordyline, Fatsia, Fatshedera, Hosta, Mahonia, Palm, Phormium, and long branches of *Beech, Cotoneaster, Elaeagnus* and *Grisilinia*.

- Suitable twigs and stems could include:
  Angelica, Bamboo, Birch, Cornus (red and green), *Hazel* (including contorted hazel), *Willow* (various forms and colours), etc. Branches of flowering shrubs in season such as *Forsythia, Philadelphous* and *Weigela*.

- Other suitable plant material could include:
  Large fruits, vegetables, dried seed heads, sisal, spathes, driftwood, bark, roots and many more.

Newport Floral Society

Photo: Veronica Coe

Staging in Stately Homes and Large Venues

The excitement and apprehension of being invited to stage a grand design in one of our stately homes or exquisite buildings is a memorable opportunity that should be savoured and cherished.

The first approach to such a design would be to view the location in advance and consider all the elements of the surroundings such as

COLOUR, texture, scale, *shape*

and all the possibilities of design, making quick sketches of the area with measurements and taking note of what the organiser has actually asked for. This request is not always the best design for the allocated space, but consultation and negotiation will achieve a stunning piece of floral art. Visual impact is one of the most important factors to consider, whilst still managing to create actual balance and harmony with the surroundings. This theory will generally help achieve that drama and wow factor that will make a distinctive design.

The mechanics of any large scale design are even more important than those in a smaller arrangement, and it depends on the actual creation you are aiming to achieve as to what mechanics are best; using chicken wire as a covering support to hold foam in place and to help prevent it splitting with large plant material is a good idea, or you may even rely solely on chicken wire to position your plant material directly into water filled containers.

Picture 1 (overleaf top) shows a traditional fresh garland which can be made from a combination of chicken wire and wet foam, it could then be filled with large *hydrangea* heads, *lilies*, *peonies* and foliage to adorn the balustrades of a Castle entrance, you can obviously make this any size or thickness and it is extremely adaptable as a structured base for many varied designs. It can be draped, made into swags, wrapped around a pillar or just placed on the ground, thin polythene can be attached to the reverse for protection and assistance with water retention. It is sometimes advisable to position small clusters of damp moss between the chunks of foam to prevent splitting when you wrap this design around something, this will make the structure more pliable.

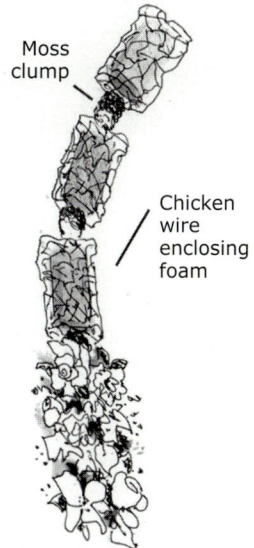

Moss clump

Chicken wire enclosing foam

Mechanics of large-scale garland

Picture 1, Derek Armstrong, Clint Harrison and Helen Hindle   Photo:
                                                                 Derek Armstrong

Derek Armstrong
Photos: Derek Armstrong

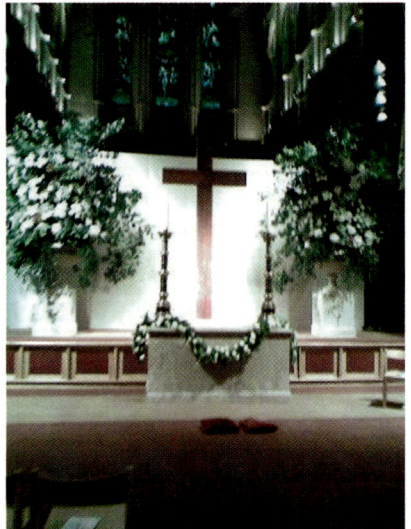

Imagine a pedestal design for a
large church in London, it could use
as many as 2500 white 'Avalanche'
Roses, white *Hydrangea* heads,
white 'Caroline Tensing' *Lilies* and
mountains of beech foliage. It could
tower approximately 25feet into the
air and would have to be created in
an urn with a three level stand fitted
inside, filled with chicken wire and
with deep water tanks attached onto
each level of the stand, everything
would then be positioned directly
into water, creating a huge all round
display.

Some events may require a camouflaged walk way; to create this 6ft x 4ft sheets of plywood could be used covered in chicken wire stapled in place, then the whole construction covered with fresh cut *buxus* foliage wedged in between the wire squares. Once completely covered these would then be trimmed with shears and by joining many together for the desired length it would form a fabulous box hedge walkway leading to the entrance of the venue. This obviously would have no water supply but it does make a stunning wall of foliage that is often used in the contract world. The freelance floral industry that works for companies in London and abroad rarely use foam as a base but prefer to use a structure of shaped wood or a chicken wire support as described above.

Picture 2 (overleaf) shows two huge columns of fresh flowers outside the entrance of a building, these could be constructed on site using a tall column of wood cemented into the square white planters, the wood in both being surrounded with chicken wire and as many as needed plastic tubes would be attached around the structure and then filled with water.

Wooden post

Chicken wire enclosing post

Tubes attached to wire

Large clusters of foliage are fed in to give a foil to build upon, this done start to fill in with flowers into the same tubes, positioning the lilies and roses in bunches of four or five together, finishing off by placing full bunches of five white *matthiola* (stocks) in clusters to complement the whole massed effect. The fragrance would be overwhelming, filling the building. This is an easy way of constructing a very dramatic pair of structures and this same technique can be used to build any size or shape, it means you can use a wider choice of flowers than normal, as shorter stems are required. Just as a covering measure you can paint the wooden stand green before attaching the wire, so if some small areas became visible it is still pleasing to the eye.

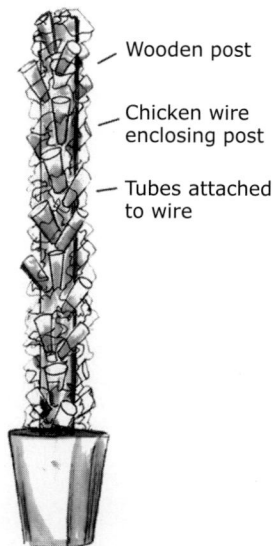

Care should always be taken to protect the fabric of a treasured building, designers work with damp materials that need to be kept alive for as long as possible, however sometimes moisture is not very welcome alongside the priceless artefacts often found in such places and one needs to be aware of this when working on the choice of mechanics. Nothing can be attached to brickwork or stand on woodwork that could hold a possible risk of damage, and care needs to be taken when spraying a finished design with water. Remember that when the designs are removed everything should be as perfect as it was when you arrived. You need to be ingenious in your approach to the structure and support

Picture 2, Derek Armstrong

Photo: Derek Armstrong

of the mechanics used, a metal G clamp and sheet of expandable foam rubber gives a grip to perhaps anchor onto a mantle shelf or a ledge, covering it with clear plastic sheeting before starting, this can always be covered with plant material and nobody will ever know how the design is kept in place.

The location of a design can sometimes mean that artificial materials and fruits have to be used, particularly if a piece of work is to be suspended from a great height and the actual visibility is diminished, this does not mean you can use poor quality materials, but sometimes a very good look alike can serve the purpose well. Imagine being asked to suspend a sphere from the inside of a tower or tall roof void in a stately home, the height of the design would mean that nobody could tell the selection of good quality materials were artificial, the design could be completed by wrapping and intertwining the whole thing with vines, most materials being man made means that weight is not an issue and it could be prepared in advance. The construction could be of any size based on a large sphere made from willow twigs densely interwoven, pads of dried moss can be added to give some textural relief and could be seen from a distance. A light design would give no logistical problems in getting it suspended. The same design made in fresh materials with no weight factor taken into account would mean the addition of reinforced hanging mechanics.

Bob Harris and Katherine Kear   *Photo: Katherine Kear*

- Often the style and theme of the building or the décor and tastes of the owner can be reflected in the designs
- Anything is possible if you plan well ahead. Think large enough
- Make it achievable for yourself
- Work with very secure mechanics
- Be organised and prepared
- Have all equipment to hand
- Use fantastic plant material
- Then the WOW factor is achievable time after time!!

Marquees

The challenge of the marquee to the flower arranger is a completely blank canvas offering the opportunity not only to decorate the marquee but also to include a grand garden or historical site in the surrounds.

A marquee can be an extension of an existing building or it can stand alone. Possibly weddings are the most common use for the marquee but it can be suitable for many other occasions e.g. themed parties, corporate occasions and family celebrations.

Regency Events Ltd Guernsey

Having a marquee in your own back garden can be convenient and personal. It gives the family the opportunity of staging an important event at home and to entertain a large number of guests without domestic disruption.

As with every location to be decorated it is important to be aware of the type of marquee chosen. Some may not have poles to support the canvas others may and these lend themselves well to hold hanging designs.

Katherine Kear
Photo: Katherine Kear

Katherine Kear   Photo: Katherine Kear

Some marquees have wooden flooring some do not, but in all cases the stability of the designs chosen is of prime importance. Windows in the marquee will give a clear view of the landscape beyond and the arranger can link this to the interior.

Many marquees have coloured interiors and some hire companies can also provide covered chairs, and these can harmonise with flowers or accessories within.

Regency Events Ltd Guernsey

Lighting inside the marquee will have an effect on the floral designs and it is important to check the type of lighting with the hire company.

One of the problems associated with decorating marquees is the temperature within the tent particularly in the summer. For this reason careful consideration must be given to conditioning the flowers and their longevity. Flowers with large blooms e.g. *agapanthus, anthurium, cymbidium orchids* and *hydrangeas* and large pieces of foliage e.g. *palms, monstera* leaves and *phormium* will provide lasting impact. In today's floral world glass containers on the tables will give a lightness and freshness to the area.

Katherine Kear
Photo: Katherine Kear

Decorating the Marquee Poles

A tent pole provides an interesting element to decorate and the resulting design will add elegance to the interior. There are several ways to do this. If you are inexperienced in decorating marquees there are many simple commercially produced mechanics on the market to help you produce your designs.

- Spray tray attached to the pole (see fig 1)
- Garlands going round the pole (see fig 2)
- Hanging baskets suspended from a central pole
- Foam rings attached to the pole (see fig 3)
- Woven cornucopia attached to the pole (see fig 4)

Fig 1

Fig 2

Hook 'simply garlands'© cages together. Secure with wire or run a piece of string through the cages so that they do not come apart. Attach wire for hanging to pole.

Oasis 'simply garlands'©

Garland on front of pole

Garland around pole

Fig 3

Foam rings attached to pole

Oasis© foam frame ring

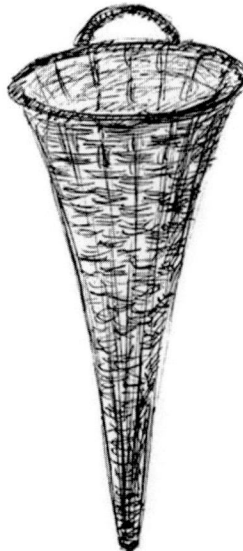

Fig 4

Woven cornucopia

If you are experienced you can cut the costs by making your own mechanics provided you have sufficient time to do this.

Fabric draped round the pole will also help to create a theme, this could be in terms of colour or subject.

Other Forms of Decoration

A large-scale design at the entrance to the marquee is very welcoming. A large statue, urn or trees or even large flowering planters on each side of the door is effective but attention must be paid to adverse weather conditions and making sure that physical balance is achieved.

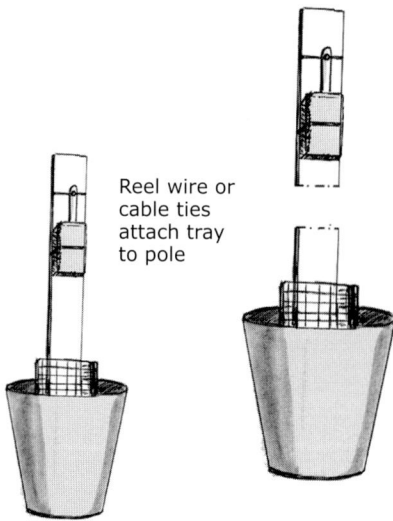

Reel wire or cable ties attach tray to pole

Foam sphere attached to top of post, covered with chicken wire and covered in leaves

Birch pole set in cement/ plaster in pot

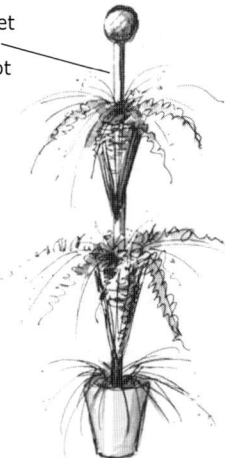

Add lots of grasses at the base of the design.

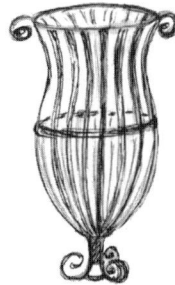

Metal urn

can be placed on a

plinth

Taller designs can be weighted
inside with bricks for stability.
Large pieces of wet foam will
also help with stability.

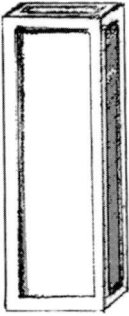

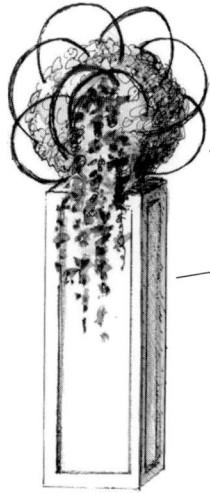

Large foam sphere
covered with *buxus*
foliage and flowers

Cage in looped
flexigrass

Trailing *amaranthus*
covers the front of
the container

Trellises and arches are another good way of making large-scale entrance
designs, while tall heavy containers rather than slim pedestals provide
the stability needed within the marquee. A further example of an
archway construction is covered in the chapter on large scale mechanics.

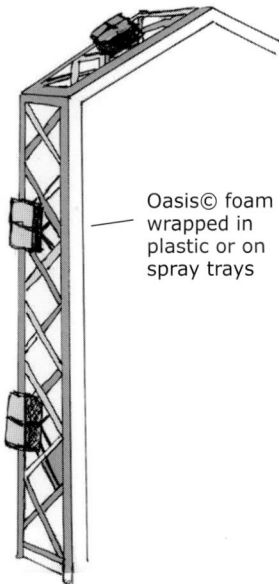

Oasis© foam
wrapped in
plastic or on
spray trays

Oasis©
foam

Trellis frames are light and portable. As they can be unstable make sure
that they are secured with their own feet or set into weighted containers.

Elizabeth Graham

Photo: Chrissie Harten

Fresh Ideas for out in the Open

Outdoor events provide exciting and challenging opportunities for the flower arranger. Familiar designs can be adapted to withstand the elements, secure mechanics are, as always, of great importance and scale requires attention to ensure that the arrangements do not get overlooked.

Doing flowers outdoors can be fulfilling and also tremendous fun!

These events by their nature call for special designs that must be constructed to withstand the elements. Our climate can be unpredictable with bright sunshine and stormy rain showers alternating within a short space of time, providing a challenge for the designer. The duration of the event will also determine the mechanics and plant material used. While the designs may be placed to enhance the outdoor settings they will need to have impact if they are located in the larger landscape. The level at which they are displayed may cause problems with maintenance or damage by people or wildlife at lower levels. Health and safety may also be an issue and has its own chapter in this book.

Entrance to the Venue and Rural Themes

A design at the approach to an outdoor venue can provide an attractive welcome for visitors. The theme of the design can be linked to the event and should also fit in with the setting.

Fallen pillars at the entrance to a rural conference centre provided the inspiration for this design in which metal mesh cages were placed to echo

Ann Traynor and Mary Pearson   *Photo: Mary Pearson*

the lines of the pillars. They were filled with 'Red Rooster' potatoes and pink *Phormium* leaves were attached to the top of the cages to pick up the colour of the potatoes.

Agricultural shows and outdoor sporting venues may provide an opportunity to introduce environmental flower designs.

A horizontal design constructed on a foam bar with threaded peppers and forms made by winding wool, *Rubus*, skeletonised raffia and wire on to willow might mark the way to a summer barbeque.

Pat Leahey
Photo:
Lyndon Parker

Garden Parties and Other Celebrations

Garden Parties are among the most popular grand outdoor events of the summer season, usually held in splendid surroundings. Parties often follow summer graduation ceremonies on the lawn; alternatively indoor events may be preceded by an invitation to drinks on the lawn if weather permits. Floral designs at these events can provide a talking point.

It may be possible to make use of garden features such as trees and statues as part of the mechanics for the designs.

Here a hammock was suspended between two birch trees for the local Agriculture College Graduation Party. A length of copper mesh wire was joined at both ends to lengths of *Salix matsudana Tortuosa* and attached to the trees with fine rope. Lengths of coloured *Salix* were woven into the structure along with *Phormium* flowers and *Rumex*. *Yucca* flowers were wired and attached to the ends of the hammock to provide a fringe and finish the design. These were long lasting materials that would survive sun and rain.

Mary Pearson   Photo: Mary Pearson

*Ann Traynor and
Mary Pearson
Photo: Mary Pearson*

A gazebo in a quiet corner of the garden provided the ideal setting for
a traditional triangular design of summer flowers and garden foliage,
Hydrangea, Delphiniums, Roses, Gerbera and *Gladioli* were arranged with
Cornus kousa, Hosta and *Roses* from the garden.

Outdoor Performances

There is a long tradition of outdoor performances in the summer and the
number of such events increases each year. From Opera in the park to
Jazz in the garden, open-air Theatre performances and outdoor Concerts,
all call for flower designs that will fit in with the theme and enchant the
audience on their way to the performance. Mature trees along a pathway
leading to a venue provide a good backdrop for designs and may serve
as way markers.

Ann Traynor and Mary Pearson   *Photo: Mary Pearson*

Here chicken wire was sandwiched with *Sphagnum moss* and formed into bands that were securely attached to the tree trunks by wiring the ends together. Well-conditioned, mature *Hydrangea* florets were then tucked into the wire. At a lower level *Phormium* leaves were loosely plaited, the ends brought together with wire and the binding point disguised with a *Gerbera* head in a small covered phial. A group of 'musicians', metal garden ornaments, stand in a pool of *Peonies* and *Rose* heads pinned into moss and chicken wire at ground level.

In this design for a performance of Shakespeare's 'King Lear' a stone sculpture of a head provided the inspiration for a floral teardrop with the quotation from the play:

'When we are born we cry that we are come to this great stage of fools.'

A length of copper wire mesh was formed into a teardrop shape, moulded to fit the contours of the face and left to flow along the undulating slope of the lawn. Leaves of *Rubus tricolor* were layered, reverse side up, under the wire which was then securely pinned to the ground with wire hairpins. The design was completed with *Chive* and *Allium* flower heads and *Delphinium* flowers. With careful spraying it kept fresh for the duration of the event.

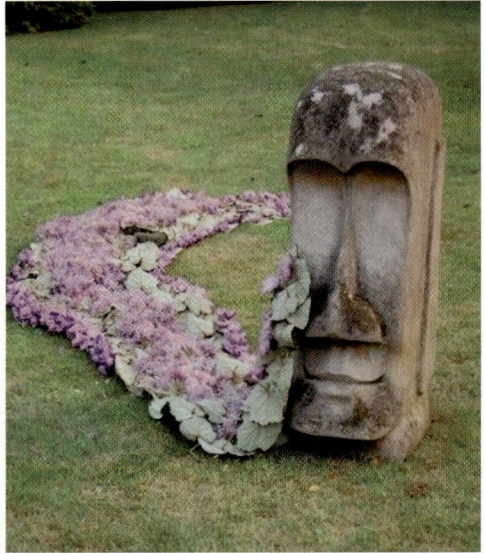

Ann Traynor and
Mary Pearson
Photos:
Mary Pearson

Ann Traynor and Mary Pearson   *Photo: Mary Pearson*

Private Parties at Home

Private parties held outdoors at home give opportunities to decorate familiar areas with special flower designs. Alcoves, niches, decking, patio tables, even swimming pools are ideal locations for these designs.

Ann Traynor and Mary Pearson   *Photo: Mary Pearson*

This urn, placed on a plinth contains a delightful collection of garden flowers and foliage including the pink flowered *Sambucus nigra* and *Rosa* 'Rambling Rector'. It provides a welcome to guests as they pass the door and enter the party in the garden.

*Southwell Flower Club
Photo: Oliver Gordon*

Rafts of willow
on foam rings,
decorated with
flowers float on a
pool.

The picture below
shows alternative
mechanics of a
pallet and plastic
containers as floats.

*Oxfordshire
Federation WI
Photo:
Catriona Karney*

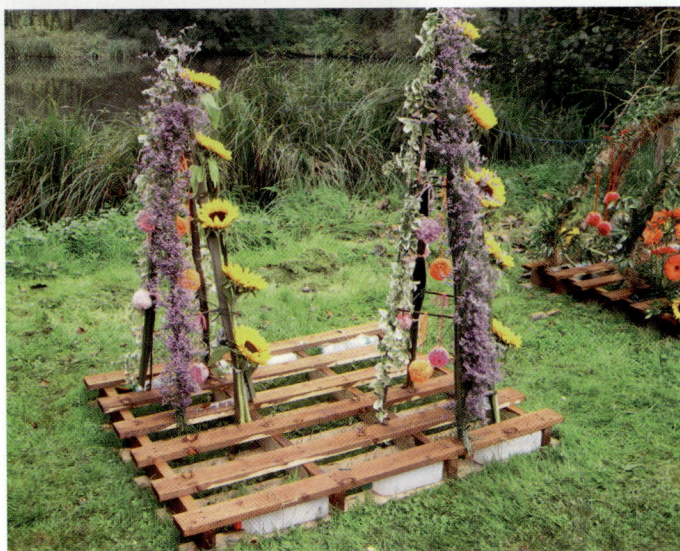

Cars and Launch Parties

Car bonnet designs have become popular and are an ideal way to arrive at an outdoor event in style. They may also be used to decorate vehicles at open-air promotions.

This design was made first and then attached to the car when complete. Long strips of thin card were covered in *Phormium* foliage using floral adhesive and corsage magnets placed between the leaves and card to ensure that they could be securely fixed to the car.

Garden roses to tone with the colour of the car were individually wired and joined in a spray to the leaves, taking great care to cover the wires and avoid scratches to the paintwork.

Incorporating decorative aluminium wire shapes, ribbons, placuna shells or woven grasses could make more elaborate designs.

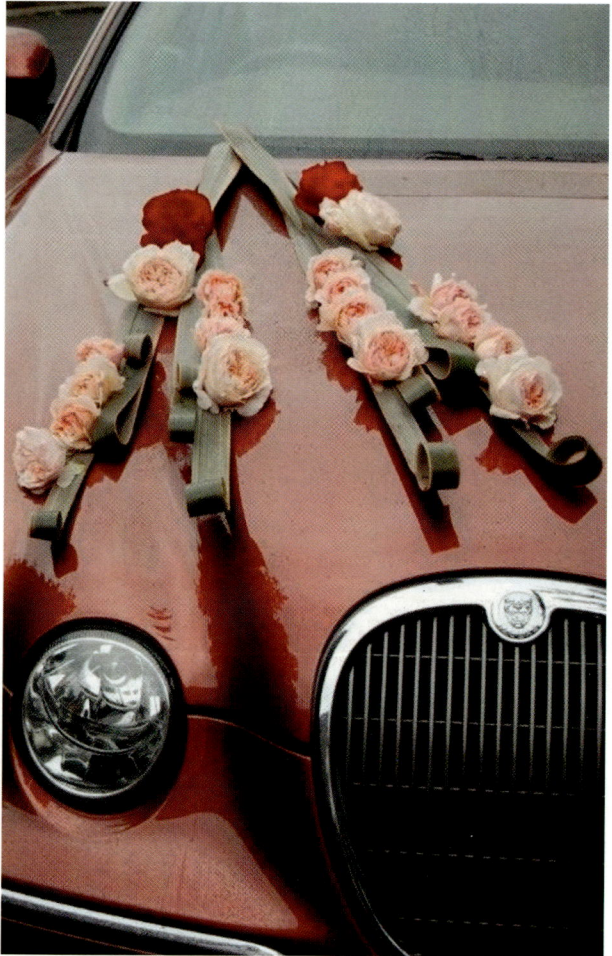

Ann Traynor and Mary Pearson
Photo: Mary Pearson

N.B. if the car is to be driven a distance or at speed additional wires may be necessary to secure the design and great care must be taken to secure all components and tape all wires to avoid damage to the vehicle.

Seasonal Designs

Until now the focus has been on summer events, however darker days should not be overlooked. Some autumn and winter events are held outdoors particularly at Halloween and Christmas. After dark an outdoor design lit up with candles or lights can be spectacular. Flowers will last longer in cool conditions and seasonal berries and leaves can be used.

Ann Traynor and Mary Pearson   *Photo: Mary Pearson*

In this design railway sleepers bordering a path have been incorporated in an autumnal design which could also be adapted for Christmas. Apple tree prunings from the orchard have been woven into a spiral construction at the base of the sleepers and red *Rhododendron* leaves and *Rose* petals added for colour. Small lengths of copper mesh wire were attached to the sleepers and *Parthenocissus* leaves and *Skimmia* berries inserted in the mesh along with conifer to add texture and provide colour contrast. Red metal cones containing candles randomly placed in the spiral light up the design and highlight the pathway for partygoers or carol singers.

Health and Safety

It is difficult to imagine how the Aberfan disaster could be linked to what flower arrangers need to be aware of in the involvement of large-scale events. The disaster which resulted in the deaths of 144 people, 116 of them children led to the establishment of the Health and Safety at Work Act of 1974, the primary piece of legislation covering occupational health & safety in the United Kingdom. Previously the Factories Act in the 1940's had tried to address some of these issues, however, this new act was much more prescriptive and laid down rules, which if transgressed could lead in some cases to legal prosecution. A Health and Safety Executive is responsible for enforcing the Act and a number of other Acts and Statutory Instruments relevant to the working environment.

In 1999 the Management of Health and Safety at Work Regulations was introduced and the basis of this was that every employer shall make a suitable and sufficient assessment of the risks to the health and safety of their employees while they are at work. The employer must also consider the risks to the health and safety of others not in his employment but who may be directly or indirectly affected by work activities. This is achieved by carrying out risk assessments to identify and manage workplace hazards.

Flower arrangers are of course not employed to decorate a stately home or compete in a National show but risk assessments are required because they are affected by any activity in the workplace. NAFAS has its own risk assessment form with guidelines for its completion and this may obtained from Headquarters, but remember other venues may wish to have the use of their own, which may be of a slightly different format. However, the same principles apply:

Photo: unknown

- A risk assessment is based on an activity NOT an environment
- You need to look at what is likely to cause harm
- How likely this is to happen
- The controls or precautions to reduce the risk.

In all of this the bottom line is to BE REASONABLE. Assessing an activity using scissors would not be considered as a high-risk activity if the working group consisted of area demonstrators, however the risk rating increases considerably if the group is disabled children!

Each risk assessment should contain four items for consideration:

- The hazard/task
- The risk
- The level of the risk
- Precautions/control

It is worth remembering that a hazard means anything that can cause harm and a risk is the chance, high, medium, or low that somebody will be harmed by the hazard.

The risk assessment for the National Show in Edinburgh 2008 identified one of the high-risk hazards as injury to demonstrators, staff and visitors from trips slips and falls resulting from water spillage and equipment. Precautions to reduce the risk were as follows:

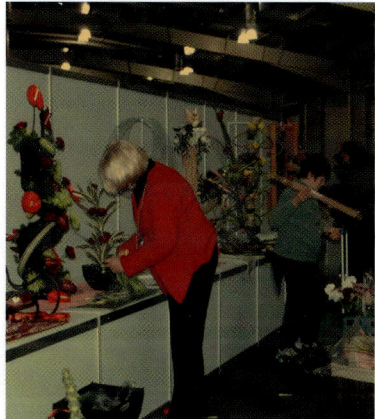

Photo: Carolyn Rutland

✓ Good working lighting at all times
✓ Rubbish to be removed and bagged timeously
✓ Spilt water or other liquids to be cleared and area marked as a hazard until dry/safe
✓ Rubbish and debris to be moved at the end of the demonstration

Similarly the use of electrical equipment and cables was identified as a low risk to demonstrators, staff and visitors. The precautions here were:

✓ All mains powered electrical equipment to have current PAT certificates. PAT= portable appliance testing
✓ Designated area for use of glue guns
✓ Extension cables to be taped to the floor

Although the risk assessment as previously mentioned looks at an activity, different venues will have their own impact on that activity. Setting up floral decorations in a marquee without a solid floor introduces the hazard of uneven ground, whilst decorating a stately home must risk assess the damage to precious objects from water and trailing objects.

Fire Safety

This is of primary importance whether the event is taking place in the village hall or in a mansion. The organising committee must be aware of local fire arrangements within the building and communicate this to all involved. Just as all club chairmen are now required to point out fire exits to members at a flower club meeting this sort of information needs to be filtered down to every person using the building for a large scale event.

The golden rules for procedure when hearing the fire alarm are:

1. Stop work immediately
2. Follow the evacuation route and proceed to the designated assembly area
3. Do NOT use the lifts
4. Use the fire exit staircases
5. Do not re-enter the building until told to do so by the person in charge

Of course all this depends on whether you have been made aware of the fire evacuation procedure and have located for yourself the fire exit routes. How many times does one sleep in a strange hotel and not look at the fire evacuation procedure on the back of the bedroom door? It is also a responsibility to make sure one does not impede the Health & Safety efforts of the venue's teams. Never block a fire exit, it is very tempting to find a space out of the way for buckets of flowers, but the area around the fire exit must be left clear because it is a fire exit! Fire doors should be kept closed and not wedged. Report anything untoward to the organisers, water spills, foliage on the floor or trailing cables being the most common.

Heights

One of the most common worries for flower arrangers is working high up. While arranging at an area festival a colleague told me that she was almost suspended from the ceiling to create a design. Michelangelo eat your heart out! Nowadays we have regulations for working at heights to ensure that this is not allowed to happen!

Arrangers Basil and Muffet Hart
Photo: Jenny Bennett

Ladders may be used up to a height of 2m, after that scaffolding should be used to work any higher. As with everything there are a few questions to be asked to make the task safer:

1. Can the job be done more safely in a different way?
2. Can the ladder be securely fixed against slipping outwards or sideways?
3. Is the site exposed (to weather, movement of persons or vehicles)?
4. Has the ladder got a safe handhold and is it close to the area of work?
5. How experienced are the users?
6. What is the nature of the surface on which the ladder will rest?
7. How much extra weight will the ladder be required to take?

Photo: unknown

8. For safety's sake always have someone holding the bottom of the ladder.

Photo: unknown

Wherever flower arrangers work, be it in a large venue or at home there are numerous issues to be aware of, but personal safety is of paramount importance. Dangerous materials e.g. aerosol sprays are often used and we should be aware of the dangers to ourselves and people around us. An aerosol spray should never be used in a confined space. It comes under COSHH regulations - the control of substances hazardous to health, and should have a COSHH assessment. The tiny particles can cause breathing difficulties to people with chest complaints.

Arrangers moving large objects, stands, boxes of flowers and ladders should be aware of the principles of manual handling:

1. Always make sure you are capable of carrying a load. If necessary divide into two and distribute the weight. Make two or three trips rather than carrying everything at once!

2. When lifting bend your knees, keep your back in line, your feet apart and hold the load close to your body using a firm grip.

Watch that back

Scissors where they should not be

3. Do not carry full buckets of water in the car. Anything containing water should be securely wedged. Do not try to replace an arrangement that has toppled over as you drive round a roundabout. This distracts you from driving.

4. Have good access to the workplace and use trolleys to keep lifting to a minimum.

Setting the perfect example

First Aid

Large venues should have a designated first aider who should be called upon whenever an incident occurs, be it a sting from an insect hiding in some flowers or someone toppling from a ladder. Never try to deal with an emergency on your own. If no one qualified is available always dial 999. It is better to call the paramedics than waste time deciding what to do. Normally the venue will require you to complete an accident form for their records, but at a large NAFAS event it would be a good idea for the organisers to have their own separate accident book also.

Opinions on Health & Safety and the usefulness of its rules and regulations vary enormously. Some question whether it is too prescriptive and does not allow one to be free to take risks. Whatever the views on this remember that these rules and regulations are there to protect us in the work we do, which can sometimes be very dangerous, and this protection is the law!

Wherever you are working keep yourself and others around you safe and secure so that the enjoyment and pleasures gained from flower arranging are not marred by unnecessary accidents.